C++ and Linux Operating System 2 Bundle Manuscript

Essential Beginners Guide on Enriching Your C++ Programming Skills and Learn the Linux Operating System

Series: Hacking Freedom and Data Driven (Senior Edition) & C++

By Isaac D. Cody

C++ PROGRAMMING & LINUX OPERATING SYSTEM

Essential Beginners Guide on Enriching Your C++ Programming Skills and Learn the Linux Operating System

ISAAC D. CODY

QUICK TABLE OF CONTENTS

This book will contain 2 manuscripts from the Hacking Freedom and Data Driven series. It will essentially be two books into one.

The first part of this book will dive into learning the sophisticated programming language of C++ and get you on your way to program like a boss!

Hacking University: Senior Edition will start your journey and conquer the world of the Linux Operating System

C++: Learn C++ Like a Boss

A Beginners Guide in Coding Programming And Dominating C++. Novice to Expert Guide To Learn and Master C++ Fast

By: Isaac D. Cody

C++
LEARN C++ LIKE A BOSS
A BEGINNERS GUIDE IN CODING PROGRAMMING AND DOMINATING C++

Novice to expert guide to learn
and master C++ FAST

ISAAC D. CODY

within this book are for clarifying purposes
only and are the owned by the owners
themselves, not affiliated with this document.

Table of Contents

Chapter 1: Basic Background, History, and the Fruition of C++

Chapter 2: Let's Begin

Chapter 3: Diving more into Program Comments, Data Types, Lines, and Characters

Chapter 4: Arrays, Loops, and Conditions

Chapter 5: Working with Operators

Chapter 6: Constants and the various types of Literals

Conclusion

Bonus: Brief Hacking History and Overview

Chapter 1: Basic Background, History, and the Fruition of C++

Before we get into how to start using C++, you have to learn what it is, and how it came about. The reason for this is simple. To truly know something, you have to know everything you possibly can learn about the subject, especially when it comes to something so technical such as computer programming.

C++ is a very important part of computer and Internet history. It is simply something that is interwoven within the history of the technological world, as we know today. Furthermore, the apps and other functions on a smart phone would not exist if it were not for C++.

When you are learning C++, you will be filled with wonder at the fact that one programming language can have so much impact in our daily lives. Almost every computer ever built can be attributed to a specific aspect that can be traced back to the language of C++. One of the benefits of learning this language is the ability to learn other languages with ease. Having the ability of learning C++ will enhance your knowledge of other programming language, which is why many people regard it as the 'godfather' of computer programming. Furthermore, many big companies still need programmers that have C++ as they rely this programming language to run their central computer system. So when the going gets tough, just know it'll benefit you in the long run so stay strong and get in the programming mindset!

History of C++

Bjarne Strousup was working on his thesis for his doctorate, and he decided to work with a programming language that was known as Simula. This language one one of the first programming languages of the computer age. However it was very slow and full of bugs.

Strousup came up with the idea of C with Classes. A programming language that was a lot faster than Simula. C with classes later became Cfront which sped up the process of creating a language. However, Cfront was left in the dust when C++ came along, because it added compilers into the language, making it a lot easier, and faster to use than any other project language of the time.

Since then there have been annotated reference guides and updates to the language to make it better and faster, and even easier to use. C++ for Dummies is a popular guide for this language.

C++ is one of the most popular languages out there today. This language is the best for many industries, so rather than make a new language which takes a lot of time, they just adapt C++ to many different variations because it is versatile in its nature.

Exactly what is C++

C++ is not just any programming language, it is object oriented. Object oriented programming or OOP for short, is programming that revolves around objects rather than actions. It is like looking at the whole picture at once, rather than each individual puzzle piece.

This programming language was designed with flexibility and speed in mind, as other languages of the time were way too slow, and could only do one thing, so every time you wanted to create something new, you needed a new language.

There are many things that you can use this language for, and they are still very much popular today, despite the ominous amount of languages that are out there now.

- Prepackaged scripts: These are what script enthusiasts, and new hackers use to practice their programming techniques. Since so many people nowadays want to take the easy way out, scripts that come already prepared are what most hackers are looking for, thus the packages need to improve, and they do so using C++.

- Video Games: Let's face it, pretty much everyone plays video games at some point in their life. Whether it is growing up, or when you have kids, you will get sucked into the realm of video games, and you can never escape. Those games can be attributed to some way or form from using the C++ language. If you are into making games, and bringing the world joy through graphics, then it is definitely a good idea to learn the language of C++

- Web pages: A lot of web pages are made using C++. The reason for this is because the language is so easy to manipulate, it makes for a quick and easy website that has plenty of interactive features for people. Some websites you may visit often that are created with C++ are Amazon and Ebay. If you like designing web pages you should learn C++ to be efficient and maybe even land a decent job in this field.

- Phone Apps: Nowadays it seems everyone has a smart phone, and that means apps galore. There are thousands of apps out there, and more are being made every day. Some apps are free, some apps cost money, but a good

chunk were made using C++. That is
because this language is so scalable that
it can be used for simple games and
more intricate shopping apps.

There are a lot of other minor things that C++
is used for, such as VoIP calling. That was
created using C++. The fact of the matter is,
you will get told time and time again that C++
is a dying language when in reality that is just a
ruse that JAVA people uses to scare people into
switching languages to ensure that C++ is a
dying language.

Why It's used

C++ is used not only for its flexibility and
speed, but because it has a lot of components, it
is fairly easy to learn, and if you master C++,
you can master the other languages with ease.
The reason for this is that when you learn
something that is a little more complex than
everything else first, the easier stuff will fall
right into place, however, if you get used to
easy to learn subjects, then you will find that
the more difficult stuff is hard to learn because

you are not used to putting in that much effort into the subject that you are trying to learn.

If you want to learn a language that you can use for different types of functions within the realm of computer technology, then this is the language for you. You can do almost anything with it, and once you learn enough about it, you may be able to figure out ways to manipulate the language to do things that it generally cannot do.

C++ is a very important language when it comes to computer programming, and though it has a lot of variables from the way that it is laid out, it is very easy to read, and very easy to create. This makes it one of the most desired programming languages that are out there, because no one wants to struggle to read code. No one wants to have to spend all of their time out there working on what they know is right just because they cannot find where they went wrong.

Job Outlook

Yes, there are a lot of jobs out there that still rely on C++ to operate. There are so many different things that you could do, and all of them affect other people in the community. Video game designing, and web page designing are two of the most prominent things that are out there. You could also become a white hat or blue hat hacker.

But according to payscale.com (search software engineer), a person with C++ Software engineer background can earn up to $57,000 to $120,000 based on experience. The median is around $80,363. Some other titles that people with C++ programming language have is Computer Programmer, Electrical Engineer, and Application Developer.

However, to be the best that you can be, you should always know two or three programming languages to be marketable. Though those languages will not be included in this book, do not marry yourself to a single language. Instead, just like with human language, broaden your horizons and dabble in a few, but keep one as your main language.

C++ should be the main language that you fall back on due to its versatility. Maybe use JAVA or Linux as your other languages, but C++ is the best main language to have, and you only want the best as your main.

C++ is a statically written lower level language which means that it is a clean cut expansive language.

C++ is a fully functional super set of C that supports object oriented programming. This means that it supports all the pillars of OOP, such as encapsulation, data hiding, inheritance and polymorphism.

To learn more about object oriented programming, you can do a quick search online, and find out more about it. It is best to get some knowledge about what it is, but it is not quintessential to your knowledge of C++, so it will not really be included in this book, except for a few mentions in passing, and some tidbits of information here and there.

Three Important Components of C++

The standard C++ is made up of three very important concepts.

- Core Language: This is made up of all the variables, data types, literals, and other important aspects of the language, creating building blocks to get to the next level

- C++ Standard Library: this allows you to manipulate files, and other workings within the language, and bend them to your will.

- STL: This stands for Standard Template Library, which gives you functions to manipulate data structures and variables and other things of the sort.

Why is C++ considered the best language out there?

Well, aside from the copiously mentioned flexibility, speed, and simplicity, it is a language that has spanned over thirty years, and is still widely used today. There are not many products in any genre of life out there that can say the same. Products and companies come and go, but only true perfection stays. Well that is how the saying goes. To be honest, C++ has had many updates since then, but the core process is still the same. When it came out it was light years ahead of its time, and today it is still a pretty advanced piece of technology, due to the updates that keep it on top.

There are a lot of opinions that also have to do with why C++ is considered the best. While there are a lot of people who say that C++ is no longer relevant, even more vouch that it is still the best language out there, and it is their fall back language. It is the one they know the most about, and the one they carry close to their heart. The reasons vary, but the fact that 90% of programmers default to C++ shows that it is very much the best programming language out there today.

C++ is one of the few languages that follow the ANSI standard completely, which is why some of the best games you will ever play are still written with C++. Because their compilers are set to ensure that all commands are written and executed without errors. It can also be used across many different types of platforms, whether you have a Microsoft, Unix, Mac, Windows, or and Alpha device, it is possible to use C++. This is a great thing, because a lot of programmers have to operate across many different platforms, and the universality makes it easy and portable. Just throw your code on a flash drive and upload it wherever it is needed.

Benefits of using the C++ language

There are a lot of benefits that you will be able to enjoy when using the C++ language. Some of these benefits include:

- The big library: since C++ has been around for along time, they have a library that is pretty large. This is available for you to use so you can pick out the codes that you want inside of your script and save some time and even learn some new things. You can also create some of your own codes if you wish, but this library can be really helpful for the beginner who is learning and can make it easier than ever to get the code written.

- Ability to work with other languages: C++ is a great language to use with some of the other programming languages out there. This makes it easier to really work on the projects that you want because you can add in the parts that you like from different coding languages and combine them together to get something really amazing.

- Works on many projects: most other programming languages are going to focus on just one or two little projects. For example, using JavaScript means that you are just going to be working on websites. But with C++, you are able to use it to help with a lot of different projects. Whether you are looking to work on a website, looking to create a new program, or do something else with programming, you will be able to do it with the help of C++.

- Fast and reliable: if you have used some of the other coding languages that are popular in the past, you will find that sometimes they aren't the most reliable. Information may slip through or they won't start working the way that you would like. If you want something that works the first time and is reliable, then it is a good idea to go with C++.

- Offers a lot of power: those who like to work in programming and want to have a lot of power in the work that they are doing will find that C++ is the right option for them to choose. It has some of the best power for the programming languages that are out there.

These are just a few of the benefit that you can enjoy when you are using the C++ programming language. It may seem a bit more difficult to use than some of the others, such as Python, but it has a lot of the power that you need and can work well with other programming languages. With a bit of practice, you are going to get all the basics of this language down and really enjoy what you are able to do with this programming language.

Chapter 2: Let's Begin

Let's begin! There are a lot of places we can start, but let's talk about environments first. While you do not really need to set up your own environment, as there are many online. An environment is a compiler of your choice that takes your code, and does all of the functions for you. In the old days, you would have to open your command prompts and create an environment to use, but those days are over. A simple mistake back in the day could do some serious damage to their computers. Now you can practice some risky prompts without any risk to your device whatsoever.

There are many examples to try out and use on the internet. To try them out, the easiest place to go is http://www.compileonline.com Choose the "Learn C++" option down at the bottom, and it will take you to where you need to go.

Here is an example to try. The output should be the words "**Try This**".

```
#include <iostream>


using namespace std;


int main ()

{

        court << "Use This One!";

        return 0;

}
```

Now you can choose to type these codes into the compiler directly, or you can write several, and save them to your computer, and access them whenever, so that you don't have to retype them every time you want to mess with them. You can use several different types of text editors. However, some of them are device type specific. This means they only work on the type of device that you create them on.

The text editors that you can use are OS edit command, Brief, EMACS, epsilon, Windows Notepad, vlm or vl. However, only vlm and vl are multi platform usable. Make sure to save the files with the extension .c or .cpp.

You should start in a text editor to get the rough draft going on your program before you even think of moving to a compiler. This is because once you get to a compiler, it is a lot easier to mess up on your program, and not catch it. However, if you have it laid out in a nice, clean-cut fashion in a text editor, then you should have no problems with getting things going in the compiler.

C++ Compilers

There are many different compilers out there, and a lot of them are pretty expensive. Those compilers are for the elite programmers who have mastered the lower level compilers already. Beginners only need a basic compiler, and most of those are free. However, just like with anything that is free, you have to be careful of what you are getting. There are more bad cheap compliers than good ones out there so on the pretense of being free, I would suggest you paying additional functions past the start up page. These additional functions are usually very cheap anyways so you won't have to break the bank to get them.

One of the most popular compilers available is the GNU C/C++ compiler. It is used most commonly in UNIX and Linux installations. To see if you already have the compiler, pull up the command line in your UNIX/Linux application and type in the following

```
$ g++ -v
```

If the compiler is installed, then you should see this message on the screen:

Using built-in specs.

Target: i386-redhat-linux

Configured with: ../configure –prefix=/usr ......

Thread model: posix

gcc version 4.1.2 20080704 (Red Hat 4.1.2-46)

If this message does not come up on your screen, the compiler either isn't on the computer or you installed it incorrectly and you will need to go through and get it properly installed.

In this book, we will go over how to install using the Windows platform. If you have a different platform, then you should go to http://gcc.gnu.org/install/ and read the instructions on how to download it onto your platform.

To install this compiler on your Windows computer, you will need to first install MinGW. This is the software that makes the compiler compatible with your computer, and it is very important that you have this software, otherwise you will not even be able to download the compiler at all.

To install this software, you can go to the homepage of the software at www.mingw.org and allow it to direct you to where you need to go. Once you install that you should install gcc core, gcc-g++, MinGW runtime and blnutlls, at the bare minimum, but you can install more if you would like. Once you are done with the install, you can run all of the GNU tools from the Command line on Windows.

Now that you have everything set up to where you can run it, you can start learning more about how to run the programs themselves.

Basic Syntax

C++ can be defined as not only the program, but objects that collectively communicate by invoking other methods. When you are working with C++ you should know what four things mean above all else.

Class- This is a template or a blueprint that states the object and its support type, and describes the behaviors of an object. This means that objects are sorted by their behaviors and their actions /supports into classes that fit the description of the object in question.

Object- Objects have behaviors and states. For example, if you look at a dog, it has states. These states could be classified as color, breed, name, standard of breed (AKC/AKA/APC registries). "Dogs" also show certain behaviors as well. They wag their tails, they bark, they pant, they eat dry kibble, and they go to the bathroom outside in the yard. These things make dogs a *unique object*. These objects are classified into groups know as, you guessed it, classes.

Method- This is another term for behavior. There can be as many or as few as you choose in your classes. This is where all of the data is manipulated, and actions are played out, along with the place that all of the logic is written. Methods are especially important because without them, your program would not know what it is supposed to do with the variable that you give it. It would just sit there like a dud and do nothing.

Instant Variables- These refer to each individual object. Each object is classified with a unique set of these variables that act as a fingerprint for an object. These variables are assigned to the object by using values that occur whenever the object is created.

Now that you know the four main definitions of programming, Let's take a look at a code that you can write that will print out: **"Try This"**. Unlike the example above, this will explain a little more in depth what you are wanting to do, and the reason for each function.

#include <iostream>

using namespace std;

// main() [this is when the program will begin to execute.]

int main()

{

31

```
        cout << "Try This"; // [Prints Try This]

        return 0;

}
```

This function will allow you to print whatever you want, not just the words "Try This".

Now let's break down the various aspects of the program that is set out above. There are several different aspects of this language that you have to take in consideration. Each aspect is important in getting it to run, and if you do not execute them entirely.

Headers- There are several headers out there for C++, and all of them are necessary or at the very least useful to your programming operations. However, for most functions you will see the header that is above <iostream>. When you use a header be sure to enclose it properly, and put **#include before** it to prompt the program to use that header.

Namespace- Namespaces are a fairly new addition to C++, only coming about in the 2011 update. They do not do much, other than describe which namespace to use. While they are not necessary, they save you a lot of confusion on functions of a program. It simply act as a way to organize your functions more systematically.

Main- Here is where the main function begins. Using the line // **main()** instructs the program to start executing the main function of the program, and start the out put process. It is essential that you set up the main function command, otherwise your program will not know what it is supposed to be running, nor will it know when it is supposed to run. This will be seen as a single line comment inside the program and it is going to tell the program that the main function is beginning.

INT main- This is where the function execution officially begins. If you do not include this, the entire process will stop, because you did not introduce the variables, and without the variables, the program is lost.

Cout- This instructs the program to display the message that you want on the screen. If you do not put cout, chances are your program will may or may not fail. The problem is you don't know if you succeed or not so if you want to make sure that everything runs smoothly, be sure to add cout.

Return- This returns the value back to zero, and terminates the function. It instructs the program to end the process, and go back to the beginning.

Now to compile and execute your first official C++ program.

First you must know how to *save* the file. Open your chosen text editor, and enter the code that is seen above. Once you have done that, hit save as, and choose a file location that is easily found. For organization purposes, it is always best to have a separate folder for all of your programs. Save the file as hello.cpp, and once you have saved it, you should open up your command prompt before heading to the directory where the file is saved.

To get the file to open inside your compiler, start by typing 'g++ hello.cpp'. you can then press enter and the code will be opened properly. As long as there aren't any errors, the prompt is going to generate an a.out executable file. To run the program, type out 'o.out' and see the compiler work. The information that you should get on the compiler from this on the computer includes:

$ g++ hello.cpp

$ ./a.out

Try This

Make sure that you are inputting all of the variables the proper way, and remember, these things are case sensitive. If you do not input the functions the right way, you will find that things tend to go awry. The thing with coding is you have to be precise. This detailed oriented personal attributed applies to all programming languages! However, anyone can do it if they are willing to pay attention.

The basic function commands are not the only things that you need to use. There are other things that are important when you are building a prompt as well, as they too instruct the program to do specific things. Some of these things are blocks and semicolons.

You probably think a pause in a sentence when you think semicolon, however, they are complete stops in C++ programs. The semicolon indicates the termination of a statement. This means that each individual statement must be indicated by the use of a semicolon. The following are three different statements.

```
x=y;

y=y+1;

add(x,y);
```

Each one of those statements were separated by not only a line break, but also a semicolon. You could also do it this way.

x=y; y=y+1; add(x,y);

Each one of those will be recognized as separate statements simply because of the semicolon. It is kind of mind blowing how something so simple can have so much of an impact.

In this coding language, a block is going to be a set of statements that you enclose with brackets. These statements are logical entities that the program puts on the screen due to the main command prompt. For example

```
{
        cout << "I like Pizza">>; //prints I like
Pizza

        return 0
}
```

The end of a line is not a terminator, as was indicated above. The semicolon is the only thing that terminates the statement.

Identifiers

Now let us move on to the identifiers in the program. These identifiers are used to identify multiple things, such as classes, modules, functions and variables within a block. An identifier is going to be a group of letters and numbers that you are able to name your program or your files and they must start with a letter, but can have any letter or number you want afterwards. There are no punctuation characters other than what you might see in a sentence that are allowed as identifiers. You will not see characters such as @,&,% or $, and the programming is case sensitive. That means YokoOno is different than Yokoono, yokoOno, and yokoono. Make sure that you are capitalizing only the letters that you should be capitalizing in your programs.

Though pretty much anything can be an identifier, there are some things that are reserved for keywords in C++, and can't be used as identifiers. These words are as follows.

asm		
Break	Bool	Auto
Char	Catch	Case
Const cast	Const	Class
Delete	Default	Continue
Dynamic cast	Double	Do
Explicit	Enum	Else
False	Extern	Export
Friend	For	Float
Inline	If	Goto
Mutable	Long	Int
Protected	Private	Namespace
Reinterpret cast	Register	Public
Signed	Short	Return
Static cast	Static	Sizeof
Template	Switch	Struct
True	Throw	This
Typeid	Typedef	Try
Unsigned	Unlon	Typename

Void	Virtual	Using
While	Wchar t	Volatile

Everything else is fair game when it comes to identifiers. Think of identifiers as usernames and passwords. Mix it up, but make sure that they are functional.

Trigraphs

Trigraphs are going to be sequences of three characters that will represent just one character. You will notice these because they are going to start out with two questions marks at the beginning. Seems a little redundant to use three characters when one will work, but the reason behind this is so you do not confuse the program with the meaning of the character, as many are similar.

Here are some frequently used trigraphs to give you an example of what we mean.

??=	#
??/	\
??'	^
??(	[
??)	]
??!	|
??<	{
??>	}
??-	~

Not all compilers support trigraphs due to their confusing nature, and most people try to stay away from them, however, it has been found that when you memorize trigraphs, you are less likely to mess up by hitting the wrong symbol in your function.

Whitespace

Moving on to whitespace. This is the empty lines in a program. Sometimes they contain comments, and these are known as blank lines. The compilers completely ignore them. Whitespace describes blanks, new lines, tabs, characters and comments. It is merely used to make your program look more organized and readable.

There should be at least one line of whitespace between the variable/identifier and the statement.

QUIZ

You thought that you could just waltz through this book without being tested on if you were paying attention? No cheating either! Just because you can peek at the answers does not mean that you should. You should take it just like a normal quiz to truly test your knowledge so you can figure out if you need to go back and re-read over some things. This is a short quiz, so you will be okay.

1.   What is whitespace?

2. Fill in the blanks ____ <<x=y+1_>>

3. What are trigraphs?

4. Who Invented the C with Classes language?

5. What is the header used in most functions?

Answers

1. The blank spaces or comments that the compiler ignores

2. Cout <<x=y+1;>>

3. A sequence of three characters that represent a single character

4. Bjarne Strousup

5. <iostream>

Congratulations, if you got all five right, then you can move on to the next section! However, if you got more than one wrong, then you should probably go back and reread the

section. If you're ready then onwards to
Chapter 3.

Chapter 3: Diving more into Program Comments, Data Types, Lines, and Characters

Now that we have covered the bare basics of C++ it is time to get into some more in depth subjects that surround the program. While these are more in depth, they are still a paramount concepts all beginners need to learn.

Program Comments

So, there are going to be times when you will want to write some comments inside of your code. These are important because they allow you to leave a little message inside the code so that others who are reading through it later on will be able to get a good look at exactly how your code is ran and also provide "referral" to what you're trying to accomplish in your code. Furthermore, leaving notes within the lines of your code is a good way to notify yourself where a code might have gone wrong. By putting comments inside your codes, you are more likely to know where you succeed or where you went wrong.

These comments can be as simple or as complex as you would like. Some people will just place in one or two words if that is all that is needed to help out the other users, but there are other times when you are going to need to combine a few more lines into the mix to ensure that it is all going to work out and that the other person understands what is going on inside of the code.

In this language, you will just need to use the // symbol in order to show that you are writing out a comment. You can make it as long as you would like, just make sure that when the comment is done, you skip to the next line so that the program knows that it is supposed to start reading through it again.

The program is going to stop reading after the // and it is not going to affect the way that the program works. Other programmers who look at the code will see the comments that you write, but when the program is executed, these comments are going to be skipped. You can add in as many as you would like to your program, but do try to keep them a bit limited because it can start to clog up the code and make it hard to read and understand.

Program comments are basically the statements that are inside the code. The statements, or comments, are going to be there to help others who use your code understand what the purpose of each function is. All program languages allow for some type of comments, but they do not allow all of the kinds of comments that are out there. The most common to use is a single line comment. This is what all program languages allow for. These comments are simple explanatory lines that tell the next reader what the purpose is in a simple sentence.

There are also multiple line comments. This is one that very few program languages allow for. C++ is one of those few languages. Sometimes you have a more complex explanation, and it needs to span over more than one line. This is possible to do in C++.

When you are using a single line comment, you will see that it is written out in the code with // and can go all the way to the end of your line. An example of this is:

```
{

        cout << "that's great" >>; //prints that's
great

        return 0

}
```

will have the final output of "that's great" and nothing else. The comment is ignored by the compiler so that you can let other programmers in on what the code is for, or what you need done to the code.

However if you are trying to get some help on a code, you should use a multi line comment so that you can easily get the best out of your complicated code. Multi line comments are surrounded by these symbols /*-*/. Typed out like that it almost looks like an emoji. For example

/* I need help making the puppet dance*/ is a comment. However, that is still a single line comment still. A better example would be

/* I need help making the puppet dance

*All he does at this point is sway from side to side */

That would be a multi line comment. As you can see, when you start a new line you should put the asterisk at the beginning to indicate to the program that you are still writing a comment and that the next line is indeed whitespace. When compiled it will ignore the comments and only show what you want it to show.

While you can mix the comment styles, it is best to keep them separated for now, until you get the hang of everything.

Data Types

You have to use different variables when you are writing a program using any language. These are nothing more than just reserved memory values that store locations in some space in the memory of the compiler. The above list of reserved keywords are useful here as well. While there are a lot of keywords, there are seven basic keywords that define data types.

Type	Keyword
Wide character	Wchar_t
Valueless	Void
Double floating point	Double
Floating point	Float
Integer	Int
Character	Char
Boolean	bool

Most of the data types that you can use can be modified using one of these following modifiers to help:

Long,

Short

Unsigned

Signed

Variable Types Cont...

When you are using variables inside of a coding language, you are providing some storage space that makes it easier to for the program to manipulate. All of the variables that you use will be attached to a different type and these types are going to determine the layout and the size of the memory of the variable. It is also going to set a range of values that you are able to store on this memory space.

Naming the variable is going to be similar to naming the identifier. You will only be able to name it with a letter or an underscore and the letters are going to be case sensitive. But after that, you are able to use any type of digit, letter, and character that you would like.

Again, the basic variables that you will be able to use here in more detail include:

• Wchart_t: this is the wide character type.

• Void: this is going to represent the absence of a type

• Double: this is a floating value that will have double precision.

• Float: this is a floating point that is going to have single precision.

• Int: this is an integer

• Char: this is often going to be just one byte and is a type of integer.

• Bool: this is going to work with values that are either true or false.

You can also define other types of variables. These variables are things line pointer, array, reference, enumeration, data structures, and classes.

Creating a new line

Now that you know the data types and modifiers, and all about making a comment in your program, it is time to learn about how to create a new line. This is a problem that a lot of new programmers run into. They have their program all nice and laid out in the input, but the output is still really mashed together and really unkempt. This is because they did not properly create a new line. Remember that whitespace is ignored, so you cannot just skip a line, and expect to have a line skipped in your program. You have to indicate to the compiler that you want to start a new line. This is really important, as when you play out your program, you want it to run smoothly. You do not want to see something like this.

Try This Today I ate Pizza and I did math. 6= (7-1) that what I learned today.

You would probably rather see this.

Try This

today I ate pizza and I did math

6=(7-1)

that is what I learned today

To make the distinction, you have to have the right function, as that is what programming relies on, having the correct function.

To create a line break, you have to use the function endl; this will indicate that you want a line break, and you do not even have to add whitespace if you do not want to, though it is recommended because it makes your program easier to read for a human.

For example, this:

```
{
        cout << Try This;>> endl;

        <<Today I ate Pizza and did Math;>>
endl;

        <<6=(7-1);>> endl;

        << That is what I learned today;>> endl;

        return 0

}
```

Looks way better than this:

```
{
        cout << Try This;>> endl; << Today I
ate Pizza and did Math;>> endl; <<6=(7-1);>>
endl; << That is what I learned today;>> endl;

        return 0

}
```

Can you see how confusing that would get for someone reading the code? You want your code file to be easy to read, so that if someone else has to fix something, they can easily find where the mistake has been made. If everything is all jumbled together, then they would not be able to find anything very easily, now would they?

You can also indicate line breaks by using /n This is the same thing as endl; but is a lot faster to type. You can use whichever method you want but choose one and stick with it.

The importance of the basics of C++

I know what you are thinking, why must you know all these nonsense tidbits of information when you are just beginning, and the reason is, if you don't learn them now, you won't think that you will need them in the future, and then when you are reading a program that someone else wrote, you will be wondering what all of those extra characters mean, and why there is so much whitespace. Creating a habit of these simple yet somewhat tedious tasks is paramount if mastering more complicated programming methods. Just like mastering any sort of language, you have to master the basics to master the expert level concepts.

Variable definitions

A variable definitions instructs the compiler how much and where to store and create the variable. It specifies the data type and lists one or more of the variables of the type. For example

type variable_list;

You have to have a valid data type that is listed above. They may contain one or more identifier names as long as they are separated by commas, such as

int ---- j,k,l;

char----c,ch;

float---- f, salary;

double--- d;

Each of these abbreviations instructs the compiler to create variables of that type with those names. Variables can be assigned with an initial value, by indicating such with an equal sign. For example

```
#include <iostream>
using namespace std;

int. main ()
int j=10;
int k=5;
int l=j+k
{
        cout <<l>> endl;
        return 0
}
```

You should get the answer 15

You can also declare and define the variables in your program, but that is some higher level stuff, so if you would like to look into it you can google search a tutorial on that.

QUIZ

Here is the set up. You should have one phrase, a math problem, and then the answer to the math problem using said integers. You can make up all of the variables yourself, whatever you want them to be.

```
#using <header>
using namespace std;


int main ()
int _=_
```

```
int _=_

int _=_+_

{

        cout < "";> /n

         < "";> /n

        cout  < "int_";> /n

        return 0

}
```

Simply enter your digits in and make sure your numbers add up. After you've done so, rerun the code without relying on copying and pasting the code without the intergers. This way, you'll have a basic understanding of variables and playing with the basic integers operations within C++.

Chapter 4: Arrays, Loops, and Conditions

Believe it or not, you've learned so much already. The basics are really not that hard and now it's just about learning about a few more things and putting concept after concept together to make sure you're becoming a better C++ programmer. Let's keep going.

Arrays

Arrays are a data structure in C++ that will be able to store elements that are basically the same type and also a fixed size. Basically a collection of same type variables. Instead of using the individual variables, you would declare one array of variables such as numbers. To do this you use the numbers 0 to 99 and access each one by an index of the array.

Arrays are going to be memory locations that are continuous. The lowest is always the first element and then the highest element is going to be the last.

Initializing arrays

You can initialize arrays one by one or using a single statement. Example

double balance [5]= {1000.0, 2.0, 3.4, 17.0, 50.0};

The numbers that are found between the bracket can't end up higher than the amount of elements that you are using. This means that you cannot have six sets of numbers when your array title only specified five. However, if you do not specify the size, then an array of just the right size is created. You would type it as follows double balance [] {1000.0, 2.0, 3.4, 17.0, 50.0};

This creates the exact same array as the previous example, only you did not specify the array size so it was created for you. Pretty nifty.

Now that you know how to write an array, it is time to move on to putting it into the actual program. This program is a bit more advanced than the ones before, and has a few more elements. You can look up these elements on www.compileonline.com. You will be directed to a lot of tutorials and there is even a PDF file for you to download.

Here is the formula for your program to assign an array.

#include <iostream>

```cpp
using namespace std;

#include <iomanip>
using std::setw;

int main ()
{
        int n[ 10 ];  //n is an array of ten
integers
        // initialize elements of array n to 0
        for ( int i=0; I <10; i++)
        {
                n[i] =i+100; // set ekement at
location I to i+ 100
        }
        cout << element << setw(13) <<
value<< endl:
        //output each array element's value
        for (int j=0; j<10; j++)
        {
                cout << setw(7)<< j << setw(13)
<<n[j] << endl;
        }
```

```
    return 0

}
```

This program was able to use the setw()
function in order to format the output that you
see.

Loop Types

The loop types are used any time that you
would like to take one type of code and execute
it over and over. These statements are going to
be done one right after the other. The loop
statement will make it easier to execute these
statements as many times as you would like.

There are four types of loops. These loops
handle different requirements.

While loop

The While loop is going to continue repeating the loop as long as a certain condition is met. It is going to test out this condition each time it restarts the loop cycle and will do this until the condition is no longer true.

Written like this

while (condition)

{

    statement(s);

}

For Loop

This loop executes a statement sequence over and over again while abbreviating the code that manages the loop variables.

Written like this

```
for ( init; condition; increment)
{
        statement(s);
}
```

Do.. while loop

The Do...while loop is going to be similar to the while statement, but it is going to test the condition when you reach the end of your statement, rather than the beginning.

Written like this

```
do
    {
            statement(s);
}while (condition);
```

Nested loops

The nested loop is going to have a loop that works inside of another loop, to create a continuous loop of loops. This one can get confusing after awhile.

Written like this

```
while (condition)
{
        while (condition)
        {
                statement(s)
```

```
    }

        statement(s) // you can put more
statements

}
```

Why is this important

Eventually you are going to want to branch out.
I would highly recommend to further enhance
your C++knowledge of the basics to ensure
mastery and better understanding of more
difficult tasks.

Though these may seem like they are too
advanced for some or too easy for others, it's
always good to do other practices and tutorials
to enrich your programming skills. You can
find tutorials at www.compileonline.com. It
cannot be stressed enough how much of an
essential tool this is. You have to check it out
for yourself, and find out just how useful it
really is. There are tutorials for other languages
as well, not just C++ dabble around and see
what you like.

Chapter 5: Working with Operators in C++

With any of the coding languages that you plan to use, it is important that you learn how to use the operators. These are going to help you to tell the program what you would like to do and can make dealing with your own codes so much easier. There are four main types of operators that you are able to use inside your program and they will each tell the program how to behave in a different way. Some of the operators that you will be able to use with the C++ language include:

- Logical operators

- Arithmetic operators

- Assignment operators

- Relational operators

Let's take a look at how some of these work and how you can bring them out to work well when writing code in the C++ language.

Logical operators

The first type of operator that we are going to use in this guidebook are the logical operators. These are going to help you to compare some of the parts that you are putting into the system. Some of the logical operators that you can work with include:

• (||): this is known as the logical OR. With this one, the condition is going to be true if one of your operands is not zero.

• (&&): this one is known as the logical AND. If you have two operands and they are not zero, your condition is true.

• (!): this is the logical NOT. You will be able to use this to reverse the status of your operand. So if the condition ends up being false, this sign will make it true.

Arithmetic operators

Another of the operators that you are able to use is the arithmetic operators. These are pretty much the same as using math in school. You are going to tell the program to add, subtract, and do other equations with the information that you are providing. Some of the arithmetic operators that you are able to use include:

- (+): this is the addition operator that will add together two operands of your choices.

- (-): this is the subtraction operator. It is going to take the right hand operand and subtract it from the left hand operand.

- (*): this is the operator that makes it possible to do multiplication in the C++ language.

- (/): this operator helps you to do division in C++.

- (++): this is the increment operator. It is going to increase the value of your operand by one.

• (--): this is the decrement operator. It is going to decrease the operand value by just one.

Assignment operators

The assignment operators will make it easier for you to assign a name to your variable and can help with searching for, saving, and so on with the different parts of the code that you are writing. Some of the assignment operators that you may use inside of C++ include:

• (=): this operator is the simple assignment operator. It is going to assign the value of the operand on the right hand to the one that is on the left.

• (+): this one is called the Add AND operator. It is going to add together the values from both operands and then assigns the sum of these over to the operand on the left side.

• (*=): this is the Multiply AND operator. It is going to multiply both of the operands and then gives the results over to the operand on the left side.

• (-=): this is the one that will subtract the value of your operand on the right side from the one on the left and then gives this difference to the left operand.

• (/=): this is the divide and operator. It is going to divide the value that is on the left side from the one on the right side and then assigns this amount to the left side.

There are a few other assignment operators that are available, but they are more advanced so we will just stick with some of these basic ones to help keep things in order!

Relational Operators

Relational operators can be really helpful when you are working inside of the C++ language. Some of the ones that you can use include:

• (==): this is the operator that is going to check the equality of your two operands. If they are equal, the conditions will be true.

• (>): this operator is going to check the value of your operands. If the operand on the left side is higher than the one on the right, the condition will be true.

- (<): this operator is basically the opposite of the one above. If you find that the value of your operand on the left side is greater than the one on the right side, the condition will be true.

- (!=): this one is going to check the equality of your two operands and if the values are unequal, your condition is true.

- (<=): this operator is going to check whether the operand on the left side is less than or equal to the operand on the right side. If it meets this criteria, the condition is true.

- (>=): this one is going to check if the value of the operand on the left side is greater or equal to the one on the right side. If it is true, the condition is true.

Chapter 6: Helping C++ to Make Decisions

There are times when you will need the program to make decisions for you. You are able to set it up to act in a certain way based on the information that the user puts into the computer and what you decide needs to be met for the conditions to be true. The decision making is a bit more advanced inside of this system, but you will find that is pretty easy to learn and will open up a lot of ideas that you are able to work with in the C++ system. Let's take a look at some of the things that you are able to do to help the system to make decisions on its own.

Switch Statements

The first decision that we are going to work with inside of this system are the switch statements. These statements are nice because they are going to allow you to check the equality of your variable against a set of values, or cases. The variable that you are trying to check is going to be compared with each of the cases. A good example of the syntax that you are able to use for this include:

```
Switch(expression){

        case constant-expression:

        statement(s);

        break; //optional

        case constant-expression:

        statement(s);

        break; //optional



//you can add in as many of these case
statements as you would like



Default: //Optional

statement(s);

}
```

When you are working inside of these statements, there are a few rules that you should keep in mind. First, the expression of the switch statement should be the integral or enumerated class type. In addition, it can also belong to a class that has a conversion function. With C++, there isn't going to be a limit to the amount of case statements that you add into the syntax so you can make them as long or short as you would like. Just remember that you need to have a colon and a value in each of them.

Once the variable finds a value that it is equal to, it is going to keep running until it finds a break statement. The system finds the break statement, the switch is going to stop. Then the control flow will be passed on. You don't need to put in a break statement to the cases. If you end up not having one of these, the control flow will just keep being passed on.

The if statements

One of the most basic things that you are able to do in your programs is create an if statement. These are going to be based on a true and false idea inside the system. If the system says that the input is true with the condition that you set out, then the program is going to run whatever you ask it to. For example, you set it up to have the system as what the answer to 2 + 2 is. If the user puts in the answer as 4, you could have a message come up that says "That is Correct! Good Job!"

Any time that the user puts in an input that ends up being true based on the conditions that you are setting out, you are going to get the statement to show up that you picked out. On the other hand, what is going to happen if your person puts in the wrong answer. If they put the answer as 5 to the question above, it is not going to be right and the system is going to see that the answer is false.

Since the if statement is pretty basic, you are going to find that it is not going to be prepared if the person puts in the wrong answer. At this stage, if they put in any number other than 4 for the example above, the screen is just going to go blank and nothing is going to happen. The next type of statement will go more in depth and show you how to get answers based on what the person puts into the system.

The if else statement

Now as we discussed a bit above, there are some limitations that can come up when you are using the if statement. If the person puts in the wrong answer, the screen is just going to go blank and this can be a pain with the system. Plus, there are times when the user will need to put in a variety of answers, such as when they will put in their age and you want to separate those out. Their age is not necessarily wrong, but if you just want people who are older than 21, you want to make sure that an answer comes up correctly along the way.

A good syntax to use in order to work with the if else statements include:

```
if(boolean_expresion)

{

        //statement(s) will execute if the
boolean expression is true

}
Else

{
```

```
//  statement(s) will execute if the
boolean expression is false

}
```

You are able to add in as many of these into your statement as you would like. So if you would like to have a program that set apart people in five different age groups, you could set that up based on more of the "else" in your syntax. This makes it easier to add in some other choices.

So let's keep it simple. Let's say that you have 2 +2 on the system. If the person guesses that 4 is the answer, you can set that up in the first part to be the true statement and then the message "That's Right! Good Job!" will come up on the screen. But if the user puts in the answer 5 (or any other answer than 4), you can have a message like "Sorry, that is not the right answer" come up on the screen.

This gives you a lot of freedom when it comes to taking care of what you want to do inside of your code. You are going to be able to add in some different things to the process and you can really expand the code that you are working on.

Another thing that you can keep in mind when working on these, is that you are able to add some if statements and some if else statements inside of each other. This can get a bit complex as a beginner, but with some practice, you will find that it is going to add a lot of power to the whole process and can make it easier to do some of the things that you want within this coding language.

Working with the if statements and the if else statements can make your coding experience so much better. It allows the system to make decisions based on what the user is putting into the system rather than having to be there and do it themselves. Make sure to try out a few of these different types of statements and see how they are going to work within your code and with what you want to do.

Chapter 6: Constants and the various types of Literals

This language is complex, and even though what you have learned above is enough to run some simple functions, there are so many more parts to this language that it would be a crime to not put more in depth knowledge in here to help you transition to the next step.

If you want to be successful with this language, be prepared to spend long hours working hard on it. While it is a good language for beginners as it has multiple levels of difficulties, it is also something that you have to work hard at to make it to the next level. The added effects are more difficult the more you try to learn.

Programming itself is a long and difficult process, but it is definitely worth it, as there are so many professions that you can go into that require the knowledge of C++. From game designing, to working with robots and more. If it involves technology, chances are it involves C++.

So here are some more steps that you can learn, and some more important functions that you need to know to begin to master this language.

Constants and Literals

Constants and literals are an imperative part of learning C++. They refer to data types and variables in those data types. They are constant, and cannot be changed.

They act just like any other variable, other than the fact that they are stagnant and you cannot change them. The integers that you use are known as literal integers. They can have a suffix such as U or L, and they stand for unassigned, and long. These variables are used as uppercase and lowercase and can help your processes along well.

To understand the integer literals, look at some of these examples:

032uu	//illegal: can't repeat your suffix
078 octal digit	//illegal: 8 isn't considered an
Ox_Fell	//this one is legal
215	//this one is legal
212	//this one is legal
85	//this one is a decimal
30ul	//this one is an unsigned long
30l	//this one is long
30u	//this one is an unsigned int.
30	//tis one is an int.
Ox4b	//this one is a hexadecimal
0213	//this one is an octal

Floating Point Literals

These are parts of the code that will contain an integer, a decimal point, a fractional part, and an exponent part. These can be shown either through the exponential form or the decimal form.

When you choose to use the decimal point to represent these literals, you need to make sure that you are adding in at least the decimal, although adding in the exponent is good as well. When you are representing through the exponential form, you should include either the fractional part, the integer part, or both of them. The signed exponent that you are using should also be started with either E or e.

Some of the floating point literals that you are able to use in your code writing include:

.e55   //these are illegal because they are missing the fraction or the integer

210f: //these are illegal because they don't have the exponent or the decimal

510E   //these are illegal because they have an incomplete exponent

314159E-5L   //these are legal

3.15159   //these are legal

Boolean Literals

The next type of literal that we can discuss are the Boolean literals. There are two types that you will be able to use inside of your C++ code. Basically the Boolean values are going to be shown as either true or false. If the conditions that you set out are true, the Boolean expression is going to come out as true. On the other hand, if the conditions that you set out are not met, you are going to end up with a condition that is false. All of the answers when they are Boolean will come out either true or false.

Character Literals

When you see a character literal in your code, you will notice that they are closed off with single quotes. These can be simple and use something like 'x' to tell the command or they can be much longer in length as well. These are basic things that you are able to add into your code and can make things much easier to handle.

String Literals

Another type of literal that you are able to work with are the string literals. These are the ones that will be closed off using a double quote. The string is going to contain characters that are like the character literals, including options like universal, escape sequence, and plain characters. You can use the string literal in many ways including to break up one of your lines into two, and separating out things to make it easier to read. Some of the examples of the strings that you can use include:

hello, Mother"

"hello, \

Mother"

"hello, " "M" "other"

Learning how to use some of these different parts inside of the C++ programming language will make a big difference in how well you are able to use this computer language. Have some fun and experiment with using them a bit and you will find that it is easier than ever to get the results that you want!

Conclusion

Thank you again for purchasing this book. I hope that it proved to be informational, but enjoyable. Keep this book as a guide not only for knowledge, but inspiration as well. C++ seems like an intimidating language but the more you practice it in regularity, by days, months, and years, you will achieve complete mastery of this programming language like with anything else in life. I ask you not to fret and be anxious and a problem arise, because there will be many times in which this will happen. There are numerous resources out there for you just waiting to be read of discovered and it is in your best interest to do your due diligence in learning, improving, and enhancing your C++ programming skills to the next level.

Bonus: Brief Hacking History and Overview

Many people have heard the name C++ but really think nothing of it. If you are not very technologically versed then you may think that it is about having a mediocre letter grade, but that is not the case.

Believe it or not, C++ is a hacking language, and while it is not the only one out there, it is one of the more important ones because it is versatile and also easy to use. To learn the most about C++, you have to know more about the reason it came about and that would be hacking.

Hacking

Hacking is not a new concept. For as long as there has been any type of technologies around, there have been people figuring out ways to hack them. Hacking is the manipulations and/or interruptions of any technological stream of data that is being sent from one place to another. This is done with scripts. While you can get pre-packaged scripts online, many people prefer the old fashioned way of writing their own scripts, as is gives them more flexibility to do what the want with the information. Scripts that come already set up into packages have limited mobility and are pretty visible. The goal of a hacker who truly wants to hack is to remain discreet. If you are caught, unless you have permission to be doing what you are doing, you can get in a heap of trouble.

History of Hacking

Hacking began officially in the 1970s when teenagers were banned from using the phone lines because they were trying to make free calls, and figured out how to do so. Phone hacking was the biggest thing, and continued for over a hundred years. Making calls used to be expensive, especially when the phone lines were new, so of course people were trying to find ways to save money, and usually it caught up with them. Such was the case for a man named John Draper. He was arrested for figuring out how to make long distance calls simply by blowing a note into the receiver that prompted it to make a long distance call without an operator. You could then input the number and talk as long as you wish. Genius, but illegal.

He started a revolution though. A group of young teens banded together to create a phone line that hacked the system to help people make free calls. Once this spread like wild fire, Steve Jobs decided to come up with a product that he could market that hacked the phone lines and helped people make free calls by themselves.

Big time computer hacking didn't actually start until the 1980s. However, once it began, it spread like wildfire, and there were a lot of people who thought that it would be a great idea to see what all they could do, and how they could manipulate these computers.

Types of Hacking

There are several different types of hacking out there. And while the media portrays all hackers as bad, they are not. It is not black and white either. While those are the two most popular groups when talking about hacking, there are so many categories in between, that it would not be beneficial to only talk about the two that are most known.

The two main categories that all the sub categories fall between however, are ethical and unethical hacking.

Ethical hacking is hacking that is used only for good purposes. There are a lot of people who have full permissions to hack into a system, and to find all of the bugs of the software or hardware.

Ethical hackers are the ones that are responsible for all of the bug fixes in your phone, apps, tablets, or computers. These people are hired by a company to figure out what is wrong with their systems, and find the best way to fix it. These hackers are an essential part of the hacking community.

If it were not for hackers we would not have the world wide web, urls or HTML. Hacking is an important part if done within the boundaries of ethical hacking.

Unethical hacking, however, is not within the realms of hacking that is legal with current laws. It is hacking for a malicious purpose. People who hack bank mainframes and steal people's credit card and account information and use it to drain accounts are known as unethical hacking.

Unethical hacking is the bane of true hackers existence. These people are the ones that give the good guys a bad name.

Now to go on to the terms for all different types of hackers.

- White Hat Hackers: These are the completely ethical hackers. Every thing that they do is done for good. They go thru a system, and comb it down for any bugs, and build super strong firewalls so that the systems are safe. They create anti-malware software.

- Black Hat Hacking: This is the type of hacking that you have to stay away from. With great power comes great responsibility. The great responsibility to not become prey to the temptation that is black hat hacking. This type of hacking can get you in a lot of trouble, and are immoral. Hacking government files or even other people's privacy can be tempting but will lead to heavy disciplinary actions.

- Grey Hat Hacking: These are the hackers that sometimes do bad things for good reasons. Such as Anonymous. They may hack the firewall of an sensitive information file, but they do so to expose the corruption that is going on behind the firewall. These hackers are often treated like criminals, but in reality, they can be regarded as heroes depending on your perspective.

- Red Hats: These are the bounty hunters of the hacking world. They use their hacking skills to find illegal hackers, such as black hat hackers, or grey hats that are doing bad things that they should not be doing. They then turn them over to the feds, so that the illegal hackers are arrested. There are several other terms for these hackers, but they are not very appropriate, so we shall leave them out.

- Blue Hat Hackers: These are the blue collar workers of the hacking world. They sit in a cubicle and hack away all day to find bugs for Microsoft or other major companies. They clock into a nine to five job that just happens to involve hacking.

These are the main classifications of hackers. There are also elite hackers that spend their entire life becoming the best hackers that the world has seen, and green hat hackers who don't really care about hacking, they just do it for fun. Hacking can be a very useful tool, and even become a profession if you go about it the right way.

Now it is important to note that all of these hackers are going to work in a different way, but they are going to use the same kinds of codes in order to get the information that they want from other computers. A black hat hacker is going to concentrate on getting into the system and getting the information that they need to see success while the white hat hackers are going to work to keep these hackers off the system. While they are working in different ways, they are going to use the same tools and see who will come out on top in the end.

With that said, you need to be careful about what you are doing with your hacking abilities. If you are using them to get onto a system or a network that you aren't allowed to be on, then you could get into a lot of trouble. While some people find these vulnerabilities and tell the company all about them right away, it is still a legal issue if you are on the system when you shouldn't be. The company you mess with could press charges so it is always best to just work within your own network and keep that safe rather than trying to get onto a network you don't belong.

On the other hand, if you are someone who loves to work in the computer world and you want to be able to do this all the time, it may be a good idea to work as a white hat hacker. There are many companies that hold onto private and personal information for their customers, whether it is hospital information, credit card information, or something else. They are always on the lookout for a black hat hacker who may try to get into the system and take this information and a good white hat hacker can always find the work that they need helping these companies out.

Hacking University Senior Edition

Linux

Optimal beginner's guide to precisely learn and conquer the Linux operating system. A complete step-by-step guide in how the Linux command line works

BY ISAAC D. CODY

HACKING
UNIVERSITY

SENIOR EDITION

LINUX

Optimal Beginner's Guide To Precisely Learn And
Conquer The Linux Operating System. A Complete Step
By Step Guide In How Linux Command Line Works

ISAAC D. CODY

Table of Contents

Introduction

History of Linux

Benefits of Linux

Linux Distributions

Booting Into Linux

Ubuntu Basics

Installing Linux

Managing Hardware and Software

The Command Line / Terminal

Managing Directories

Apt

More Terminal Commands

Connecting to Windows / Mac
Computers

Useful Applications

Administration

Security Protocols

Scripting

Advanced Terminal Concepts

I/O Redirection

More Linux Information

What Next and Conclusion

responsibility or blame be held against the publisher for any reparation, damages, or monetary loss due to the information herein, either directly or indirectly.

The information herein is offered for informational purposes solely, and is universal as so. The presentation of the information is without contract or any type of guarantee assurance.

The trademarks that are used are without any consent, and the publication of the trademark is without permission or backing by the trademark owner. All trademarks and brands within this book are for clarifying purposes only and are the owned by the owners themselves, not affiliated with this document.

Disclaimer

Introduction

Computers contain two functional components- software and hardware. The hardware is the physical parts that spin, compute, and use electricity to perform calculations, but software is a more virtual concept. Essentially, software consists of programming code that gives instructions to the hardware-telling the parts what to do. There is "high level" software such as Internet browsers, word processors, music players, and more. But the often overlooked component is the "low level" software known as an operating system.

Operating systems are required for our personal computers to work. At an office, or with a relatively inexpensive desktop computer the operating system used is probably Microsoft's Windows. Content creators, writers, and graphic artists prefer Apple computers because they come with the creativity-focused OSX operating system. Those two OS's, Windows and OSX, have dominated the consumer market for many years. However, an alternative operating system exists that excels in usability, customization, security, and price. OS's based off of the relatively unknown Linux meet and exceed in all of those areas, but it remains an obscure option that many people have not even heard of.

Linux is not an operating system by itself. It is a kernel, or the "core" of an OS. Just as Windows NT is the kernel of Windows 7, Linux is the kernel of "distributions" such as Ubuntu, Debian, Arch, Fedora, and more.

But why would anybody abandon the familiarity of Windows for an unheard of computing environment? Linux is not only monetarily free, but it is also compatible with a huge range of devices. Older computers, and especially ones that no longer work can be rejuvenated with a Linux OS, making it run as though it were new again.

This book will explicate upon the benefits of switching to Linux, as well as serve as a beginners guide to installing, configuring, and using the most popular distribution. Then, the terminal command line will be explained to tell how to take advantage of the OS in ways not possible in other systems. Truly there are many advantages to be gained by switching to Linux, and you just might find a suitable primary OS to use on your computers by reading this book.

History of Linux

In the early 1990s Linus Torvalds was a student in Finland. Computers of the time usually ran on either DOS or UNIX, two operating systems that were both proprietary and difficult to use at the time. Torvalds sought to create his own operating system as a hobby project (based off of UNIX), but the project quickly grew and attracted more developers. The kernel continued to transform until it was portable (usable on a variety of systems) and entirely usable for computing. A kernel is not an OS, though, so Linux was combined with the GNU core utilities to create a computing environment reminiscent of an operating system.

Then, 3rd party organizations took the base Linux product and added their own high level software and features to it, thereby creating Linux "distributions". Linux remains a free hobby project even through today, and thus the kernel is continuously receiving updates and revisions by Torvalds and the community. Throughout the 2000s, many other 3rd parties saw the usefulness of the Linux environment and they began to incorporate it into their production environments and corporations. Today, Linux is known for being highly used in servers and business settings with a small dedicated desktop following. Working towards the future, the kernel has reached a level of popularity where it will never die out. Large companies revel in Linux because of its advantages and usefulness, and so the kernel and various distributions will always exist as the best alternative operating system.

Benefits of Linux

To compare how great of an option Linux is for a computer, we shall compare it to the more familiar modern operating systems.

First, Linux is free. The background of GNU places Linux into a "free and open source" mentality where most (if not all) of the software shipping with Linux is free. Free and open source (FOSS) refers to two things- the software is both monetarily free and the source code is also transparent. FOSS differs from proprietary software in that everything is open with FOSS, and there are no hidden spyware, fees, or catches involved with using it. The software is often more secure because anybody can contribute to the readily available source code and make it better. Because Linux and most of the software you can download for it is free, it is a fantastic operating system for small businesses or individual users on a budget. Certainly no quality is sacrificed by not charging a fee, because the Linux project and its various distributions are community-driven and funded through donations. Compare this to the cost of Windows, which is often many hundreds of dollars for the OS alone. Microsoft Office is a popular document writing program suite, but it also prices high. Free alternatives to these programs exist in Linux, and they definitely compare in quality to the big name products.

Probably the largest complaint held by PC owners is viruses. Windows computers are especially susceptible to them, and even anti-virus software companies are always playing catch-up to the newest threats. Simply visiting a malicious website is often enough to infect a computer, and many users choose Mac computers because of the significantly less frequency of incidents relating to malware. Linux-based operating systems are similar to Macs in that viruses are virtually non-existent. This increased security makes switching to Linux a must for anybody concerned about privacy, security, or reliability.

Linux is very popular within corporations and government agencies.

This is because high-powered servers and critical devices will run remarkably better with Linux as the operating system. The OS is known for reliability and stability too. While a Windows computer will need regular restarts and maintenance to "freshen" it up and keep it from running slow, Linux servers can run months or even years without a single restart. IT professionals inevitably choose Linux to be the backbone of their network because of its reputation. Its renowned stability is available to consumers as well on the desktop platform, and it is definitely useful for us as well.

Perhaps the best benefit to using Linux is the speed. Low system requirements mean that computers that are normally slow and groggy on Windows will be zippy and quick on Linux. Users frustrated with computer slowdowns can replace their OS for a more responsive experience. Furthermore, Linux can be installed on older computers to reinvigorate them. So even though that old laptop may be too outdated for the newest version of Windows, there will probably be a distribution of Linux that will squeeze a few more years of useful life out of it.

Customization is a sought after feature in technology. Windows, and especially OSX, limit the amount that you can do with your operating system out of fear that the average user would break it. This is not the case with Linux, as it encourages editing and changing visuals and functionality of the OS. Of course it is not necessary, and the default configuration of most Linux distributions is extremely stable and difficult to break unintentionally. But for those that love jailbreaking, modding, and playing around with computers, Linux can facilitate the creative side and even provide curious hackers with access to tools unavailable in other systems.

And finally, Linux is compatible with a huge range of devices. Linux can run on almost any architecture, meaning it can be installed on cell phones, desktops, laptops, servers, game consoles, and "smart" devices. Hobbyists take pleasure in simply installing Linux on niche, old, or quirky devices simply because they can. For the average user, it means that Linux is probably compatible with your computer.

Overall, Linux beats out the mainstream operating systems in many areas. All of these things definitely make Linux the better choice for your computer, and you should use it to gain access to these revered features. Artists, hackers, creative individuals, small business owners, techies, non-techies, and just about everyone can find something to like about Linux. The wide range of distributions means there is something for everyone, so install Linux today to see what you can gain from it.

Linux Distributions

Installing Linux can be done in a few ways, such as burning an image of the OS onto a disc, writing it to a USB, ordering a Live CD from online, formatting an SD card, or trying one out via Virtual Box. Ultimately though you cannot just install "Linux" and have a usable OS. Because Linux is just the kernel, you will need the other software as well that gives you graphical user interfaces, Internet access, etc... As previously mentioned, "distributions" of Linux exist. Distributions are versions of Linux containing preinstalled programs and a distinctive style and focus. A distribution takes the core of Linux and makes it into an entire operating system fit for daily use.

There are a mind-boggling amount of distributions. Some have specific purposes, such as Kali Linux for hacking, Sugar Linux for education, or Arch Linux for customization. Others are more general purpose, such as Ubuntu and Debian. Getting the most out of installing Linux means you will need to understand about different distributions and make a choice as to which will work best for you. Read the following sections to understand what a few of the most popular distributions are used for.

Ubuntu is the most widely known distribution at the time of writing. Throughout the 2000's it gained popularity for being user friendly and intuitive. Based off of the earlier Debian distro, Ubuntu is very similar to Windows computers in use, meaning it is an excellent choice for the Linux newbie. Because of this, we will be installing an Ubuntu variant later in the book. Canonical Ltd is the company that actively develops Ubuntu- yearly versions updates mean that the OS is always up to date and usable with emerging technology. Despite this, Ubuntu still work on many older devices at a reasonable speed. Applications can be installed from a "store" of sorts, meaning that the beginning user does not need to understand the often complicated command line. Conclusively, the Ubuntu distro is a great choice for the first time Linux user, and you should install it to learn how Linux works without diving into the harder distros.

For more specific cases of computing, Ubuntu has various sub-distributions or "flavors". These are distros that use Ubuntu as a base but have a different focus, such as Lubuntu's emphasis on lightweight applications. Here are a few:

- Lubuntu – A version of Ubuntu designed to run on older hardware or computers with limited resources. The install file is less than 1GB, and the hardware requirements are much lower than standard Ubuntu. Use this distro for revitalizing older computers but while retaining the usability of Ubuntu.

- Ubuntu Studio – Ubuntu for artists including digital painters, sound producers, and video editors. Ubuntu studio is Ubuntu but with editing tools installed already.

- Kubuntu – Ubuntu reskinned with the KDE desktop environment. The look and feel of Kubuntu differs from the classic Ubuntu feel by providing a desktop environment that is more traditional to other operating systems.

- Xubuntu is another lightweight distro that is not as quite as bare bones as Lubuntu. Xubuntu sacrifices size and hardware requirements to provide an OS that works on old, but not too old computers. It certainly is more aesthetic than other minimal Linux distributions, and it also uses Ubuntu as a base for user-friendliness and familiarity.

- Ubuntu Server – A Ubuntu variant more suited to industrial and corporate needs, Ubuntu server can be run headless and provide functionality for other Linux systems in a network.

- Mythbuntu – A variant with TV streaming and live television programs preinstalled. This is a great distro for converting old computers into "smart TV" devices via Kodi.

In conclusion, the wide range of Ubuntu distributions mean that there is a beginner OS for everybody. It is highly recommended that you take advantage of the ease of use features and general familiarity contained within Ubuntu. It serves as a stepping stone OS, one that will gradually introduce you to Linux. Definitely install it as your first Linux experience.

Linux Mint is a highly used OS in the Linux world. "Powerful and easy to use", Mint contains FOSS and proprietary software as well with the purpose of being a complete experience for Linux beginners. While not totally Linux-like, Mint is an excellent choice for a first-time alternate operating system. It consistently ranks among the most used operating systems ever, and its default layout is very similar to Windows facilitating a smooth transition into the Linux world.

Debian is one of the oldest Linux distributions, being created in 1993. Combining with the Linux philosophy, Debian keeps stability and solidity as the guiding development principal. Certainly the amount of time Debian has been around is an indicator of refinement, so those seeking an experience free of bugs and glitches can turn to Debian. Free and open source software also has a home in Debian, because most of the software contained within is FOSS. This does not mean that you are limited, though, because there is an official repository of non-free software for proprietary programs such as Adobe Flash. Debian is a decent choice for beginners, but Ubuntu still stands as the best introductory OS. Install Debian for stability, FOSS, and a wholly Linux experience.

Slackware is an OS that goes back even further than Debian. It stays close to the original Linux intent, meaning that you will have to install your own GUI and program dependencies. Because of that fact, Slackware is mostly for intermediate Linux users, as beginners will be confused at the unfamiliar methods. However, if you want to experience a Linux distribution that is closer to the UNIX roots, Slackware can provide for you.

Fedora is an OS more oriented towards workstations and business uses. Even Linus Torvalds himself is a user of Fedora, attributing to the operating system's popularity and use. Fedora is updated very often, meaning that it is always up-to-date and on the cutting edge of Linux technology. Security and FOSS are also a focus within the OS, which is why it is commonly used on endpoint computers in small businesses. There could be a challenge with working with Fedora, though, so consider it as an intermediate OS.

Arch Linux is another distribution, but one that is mostly designed for experienced users. The OS comes as a shell of a system that the user can customize to their liking, by adding only the programs and services that they want. Because of this, Arch is difficult to set up, but a rewarding and learning experience as well. By building your own personal system, you will understand the deeper Linux concepts that are hidden from you on the higher level distributions. Install this advanced OS after becoming very comfortable with the basics.

And finally, there is an abundance of other unique distributions that are worth mentioning. In the following list, we will talk about a few of them. Just note that there are so many distributions, this entire book could be filled describing each and every niche use.

- CrunchBang – A Debian-based distribution that aims to be less resource intensive. It is simple and without some of the bloatware that some distributions include by default. CrunchBang can run fast and be efficient at computing.

- Android – The popular phone OS is actually a Linux variant. Since many phones have lower specifications than full desktop PCs, the OS is a great choice for laptops, touchscreen devices, or home media computers. Furthermore, you can use many of the Google Apps from the Play store, meaning that thousands of apps, games, and utilities are available to be used on your phone and computer. While it is not recommended as your first Linux OS, it is definitely a neat choice for experimenting with older computers or children's PCs.

- Chrome OS – Another mobile-type OS developed by Google, Chrome OS is essentially a lightweight Linux browser meant for online use. Google has this OS preinstalled on their ChromeBooks, which have lower specifications than other laptops. But the OS is really only a full screen Chrome browser, so the OS is perfect for users wanting an uncomplicated experience or a dedicated Internet machine.

- Tiny Core – An OS measured in megabytes, Tiny Core is for antique computers or embedded devices. This OS is mostly for intermediate users that have a hobby project or dedicated purpose in mind.

- Damn Small Linux – Another minimal Linux variant, this OS is

best for quick access to a Linux
command line.

- openSUSE – This is a distribution
for experienced computer users.
With many tools for
administrators and program
developers, openSUSE is the best
OS for users confident in their
skills.

Positively the number of operating
systems based off of the Linux kernel is
astounding. With a huge amount of
choices, you might be confused as to
where to start and how to install it.
When in doubt (and as we will
demonstrate shortly), install Ubuntu or
one of its variants. The OS is great for
beginners and makes the Linux
transition smoother. But as you
increase in skill and wish to learn more
about Linux, you can always install
another operating system.

Booting Into Linux

If you are ready to take the plunge into a Linux based distribution, the first thing you must do is back up your files. Overwriting the OS on your hard drive will erase any data contained within, meaning you must back up any pictures, music, or files you wish to keep after the transition. Use an external hard drive, or an online data storage site (such as Google Drive) to temporarily hold your files. We are not responsible for you losing something important, back it up!

Next we will need to choose an OS. This book will use Ubuntu 16.04 as an extended example, and it is recommended you do the same. Navigate to Canonical's official website (http://www.ubuntu.com) and acquire a copy of the OS. You will download the image from the site to your computer.

Next we need to obtain an installation media. This can be a DVD, a USB drive, an SD card, or any other writable media that your computer can read. The only restriction is that the device must be able to hold an image as large as the OS download, so 4GB should be suffice. Remove everything from the drive, as it will also be formatted.

Download a tool for writing the image file. For DVDs install Imgburn (http://www.imgburn.com/), and for flash media download Rufus (https://rufus.akeo.ie/). The most common method of OS installation is to use a 4GB USB drive, and it is more recommended. Insert your media, start the appropriate program, select the OS image that was downloaded, and begin the writing process. It will take some time, as the image needs to be made bootable on the media. When it is finished, you can shut down your computer fully.

This is the point to make double sure you are ready to install Linux. Check that your files are backed up, understand that you will be erasing your current OS, and preferably have a Windows/OSX install disc handy in case you decide to switch back. If you are indeed ready to switch, continue.

With the installation media still inserted, turn on your computer. The first screen that you will see is the BIOS / UEFI POST screen, and it will give a keyboard button that you should press to enter setup. This screen shows every time you boot, but you probably pay no attention to it. Press the indicated key to enter the BIOS setup. If you are too slow, the screen will disappear and your usual OS will begin to load. If this happens, simply shut the computer back down and try again.

Once within the BIOS / UEFI, you will have to navigate to the "boot order" settings. Every computer's BIOS / UEFI is slightly different, so we cannot explain the process in detail. But generally you can follow button prompts at the bottom of the screen to understand how to navigate. After arriving at the boot order settings, place your boot medium at the top of the list. As an example, if you used a USB drive, then you would see its name and have to bring it to the top of the list. These settings control the order in which the PC searches for operating systems. With our boot medium at the top of the list, it will boot into our downloaded Linux image instead of our usual OS. Save your settings and restart the computer. If everything was done correctly the computer will begin to boot into Ubuntu.

But if something goes wrong, try troubleshooting it with these tips:

- Primary OS boots instead of Linux – You probably did not save the settings with your alternate boot medium at the top of the list. The PC is still defaulting to the internal HDD to boot.

- "No boot media found" – Did you "drag and drop" your Linux image onto the media instead of writing it? Without explicitly telling the computer it is bootable, it will not know what to do with the data files

on the media. Alternatively, you
could have a corrupted download,
or an incomplete write. Try
downloading the image again and
making another installation.

- "Kernel Panic" – Something is
  wrong with the boot process. See
  above for the possibility of a
  corrupted installation. Otherwise,
  the image you are trying to install
  may not be compatible with your
  hardware. IF you see any other
  error messages, do an Internet
  search on them. For prebuilt
  computers and laptops, search for
  the model name and Linux to find
  other user's experiences. Finally,
  you might have attempted to
  install a 64-bit image on a 32-bit
  computer. With your next image
  download, specifically select a 32-
  bit image.

- "Problem reading data from CD-
  ROM..." – Try using a different

install medium, because some distributions no longer support CD and DVD installations. USB drives are recommended.

- PC seems to boot, but there is nothing at all on the screen – If you are using a dedicated graphics card (compared to integrated GFX from the CPU), Linux might not be recognizing it completely. Plug your monitor into the motherboard directly instead of the card.

But most of those problems are rare or simply due to user error. Linux has high compatibility and is relatively easy to install/use past the initial installation. The typical user will have Ubuntu boot successfully at this point, and they will be presented with a working computing environment.

The desktop you see is referred to as a "Live CD", which is pretty much a demonstration of the OS and how it works. You have not actually installed the OS to your hard drive yet, as it is still running directly from your boot media. It is a chance for you to test out Linux without actually removing your primary OS, so take the opportunity to explore how Linux distributions work.

Ubuntu Basics

Similar to Windows, Ubuntu has a desktop graphical user interface. Applications open within Windows that can be maximized, minimized, closed, and moved around with the top bar. Ubuntu also has a "task bar" of sorts that functions much like its Windows counterpart- icons resemble programs that can be launched by clicking on them. The "Windows Button" (called the Dash Button) on the task bar is used to open a search functionality from which you can type in the name of a program or file on your computer to quickly start it.

Furthermore, there is a bar at the top of the screen that works like the "menu" bar of other operating systems. This is where drop-down menus such as "file", "edit", "help", etc... will appear once a program is active.

Besides a few nominal differences Ubuntu functions is a very familiar way. In fact, many of the programs that you may already use on other operating systems, such as Firefox, are available and sometimes preinstalled on Linux distributions. With enough experimentation and practice, you will be able to navigate the GUI of Ubuntu as if you were a professional. Continue exploring the system, and continue if you are ready to replace your main operating system with this Linux one.

Installing Linux

On the desktop, you will see an "Install Ubuntu 16.04 LTS" icon. Double clicking it will launch an application that makes installation very easy. If you are not connected to the Internet, do so now by plugging in an Ethernet cord or by connecting to Wi-Fi from the top right icon. Select your language and click "continue". The next prompt will ask whether you would like to download updates and install third-party software during the OS installation. These options are highly recommended for beginners, so check them and click "continue".

The application will move on to another screen asking for your install method. There are various options, such as erasing the disk altogether, installing alongside your primary OS, or updating a previous version of Linux. Select an option that works best for you. If you are still hesitant about making a full switch, elect to install Ubuntu as your secondary OS. That option will allow you to choose which OS to boot into after the BIOS screen. Nevertheless, select your option and click "install now".

       While Ubuntu installs, you can specify a few other options, such as your time zone, computer name, account name, and password. The entire installation should not take too long, but it will take long enough that your computer should be plugged in (if it is a laptop). After finishing, the OS will require a reboot. Congratulations, you now have a usable Linux system on your computer. Throughout the next chapters in this publication we will focus on Linux concepts, how do achieve certain tasks, and how to further your knowledge of your system.

Managing Hardware and Software

Hardware in Linux is actually much easier to manage than hardware on Windows. Instead of downloading individual drivers for devices, most of the drivers are built-in to the OS itself. This means that most popular devices can simply be installed with no further steps involved before they are usable. Printers, networks, hard drives, and other common devices are included- fiddling with drivers is not usually needed on Linux.

However, powerful graphics cards and other specific hardware will need proprietary drivers from that company to function to full efficiency. Because although your graphics card works by default with Linux, the secret and often hidden technology within can only be fully utilized with that company's software. On Ubuntu the process is straightforward- open the "additional drivers" application and let the OS search for you. After determining whether you have the devices, it will ask you which version of the driver to use.

Follow any on-screen prompts to enable the 3rd party drivers. For any devices that do not appear, do Internet research on the manufacturer's website to determine whether they released a specific Linux driver that you can download.

Software is another aspect of Linux that excels over Windows. Much like an Apple computer, Ubuntu has an app store of sorts from which you can search through repositories of applications that are compatible with your device to download and install with just a few clicks. Just search for the "Ubuntu Software Center" from dash to open the application. From there you can browse individual categories such as "Games", "Office", or "System" for a list of programs, or you can search directly by name. After finding a program, click on it and then queue up the download by clicking "install". After authenticating yourself the software will automatically download and install. From there, the application can be run by searching for it in the dash.

Another method of installing software is available through the terminal, but we will discuss that later. Ubuntu is not totally limited to software found in the app store, because programs downloaded from the Internet can also be installed. Once again, we will touch on that subject after discussing the terminal.

Overall, managing hardware and software in Ubuntu is effortless. Whether installing a new hardware device or downloading a popular program, Linux distributions make you're computing experience trouble-free. That is not to say that Linux is wholly meant for beginners, because as we will learn Linux is definitely a great choice for power users and experienced admins.

The Command Line / Terminal

Before modern computers, hardware and software were interfaced by using keyboards exclusively. The mouse brought graphical interfaces and simplified the process, but many functions remained text-only as to not present complicated options to end users. In Linux, this process continues today. There exists the GUI that is present on most distributions, but every Linux distro also has a built-in text-based interface as well, from which powerful commands can be typed and executed. Think of the terminal as a much more powerful command prompt, because you can completely use your computer exclusively through the terminal alone. With enough knowledge, a user can actually browse the Internet, install programs, manage their file system, and more through text.

Begin the terminal by launching it from dash or by using the Ctrl+Alt+T keyboard shortcut. A purple window will open and wait for your input. You can type a command and press enter to activate it. For our first command, enter "ls". This is short for list, and it will display all of the files within our current directory. You will be able to see the files and folders in Home, Ubuntu's main user folder. If you are lost, you can always type in "pwd" to print the working directory and display the name of the folder you are currently browsing. As you learn commands, it helps to write them down as to better internalize their use.

Managing Directories

Directories, another name for folders, work the same as they do in other operating systems. Folders hold files, and you must be currently accessing a directory in order to interact with the files inside of it. You can use the terminal command "cd" to change directory and move about the file system. As an example, typing "cd Desktop" from the Home folder will transfer you to that folder. Now using "ls" will not show anything (unless you added files to the desktop). To back out, type "cd ..". Practice navigating around the file system in this fashion; cd into a directory and ls to view the files.

Because you are typing commands, Linux expects your input to be exact. If you misspell a command it will simply not work, and if you type a folder or file incorrectly it will try to reference something that does not exist. Watch your input carefully when using the terminal.

Opening a file is done with a different command – ".". The period is used to start the specified file, so if you were attempting to open a picture it could be done like so: "./house.png". Both the period and the slash are necessary, as it denotes that you are running a file within the current directory. When you run a file it will be opened with the default application assigned to the file type, so in the case of a picture it will most likely be opened in an image viewer.

You can also create and remove directories and files through terminal as well. For this example navigate to the Home directory. As a shortcut you can type "cd ~" to change the directory to your Home, because the tilde key is short for "the current user's home". Make a directory with the "mkdir" command; type, "mkdir Programming" to create a new folder with that title. You can CD into it, or you can go to the GUI and enter it to prove that you have indeed created a new folder. Now remove that directory by going Home and typing "rmdir Programming". Without hesitation, Linux will remove the specified directory. Similarly, using "rm" will remove the specified file.

      Linux has a design philosophy that many users are not used to. In Windows and OSX, the OS will almost always double check that you want to commence with an action such as deleting a file or uninstalling a program. Linux distributions believe that if you are imitating an event, you definitely mean to follow through with it. It will not typically confirm deleting something, nor will it display any confirmation messages (file successfully deleted). Rather, the absence of a message indicates the process completed successfully. While the philosophy is somewhat dangerous (because you could potentially ruin your OS installation without warning), it serves as a design contrast to other operating systems. Linux gives you complete control, and it never tries to hide anything or obscure options because they might be too complicated. It takes some time to get used to, but most users agree it is a welcome change to be respected by the technology they own.

This does not compromise security, however, because any critical action requires the "sudo" command as a preface. Sudo stands for "super user do", meaning that the user of the highest permissions is requesting the following command. Any sudo entry will require an administrator password, so malicious software or un-intending keyboard spammers cannot accidently do damage without knowing the password first. A lot of the commands we use in this book require sudo permissions, so if the command fails to complete with a message explaining it does not have enough permissions you can retry with sudo.

Apt

Learning the terminal opens up computer functions that are not available through the GUI. Also, you can shorten the amount of time it takes to do many things by typing it instead. Take, for instance, the amount of work required installing a program. If you wanted to download the Google Chromium browser, you would have to open the software center, type in the name of the program, locate the correct package, mark it for installation, and execute the action. Compare that to typing "sudo apt-get install chromium-browser" into the terminal. With that one command, Ubuntu will save you many minutes.

Apt (advanced packaging tool) is the command associated with managing applications in Ubuntu. Other distributions may use their own tool, but apt is commonly used for its large repositories and simple commands. Packages are installed with the "apt-get install" formatting, where you specify the name of the program you wish to install. In the example above we specify the Chromium program with the package name "chromium-browser". Given that you do not know every package name, there is another command "apt-cache search" that can be used to locate package names matching the supplied string. So "apt-cache search chromium" would show "chromium-browser", and you could specify the correct name to install.

The usefulness of apt extends beyond that, as you can use it to update every single application on your system with a few commands. Use "apt-get update" to refresh the repository, then use "apt-get upgrade" to have every application upgrade itself to the newest version. Windows OS users should be envious at this easy process, because updating a Windows programs requires uninstalling and reinstalling with the newest version.

As time goes by, you might need to update the Ubuntu version. Every year there is a new release, and it can be installed with "apt-get dist-upgrade".

Staying up to date with the newest fixes and additions ensures your Linux system will be working healthy for a long time. You might have even noticed that installing and updating the system does not require a reboot; a feature that contributes to Linux computer's lengthy uptimes and stability. Lastly, removing an application is done with "apt-get remove" followed by the package name.

To run the programs that we install we can either search for them from the dash, or we can just type the package name into the terminal. Typing "chromium-browser" will launch it just the same as double clicking its icon would. Some programs must be started from the command line by typing the package name exclusively because the package does not show up in a dash search. Overall utilizing the terminal is a time-saver and a great way to practice moving away from slow and cumbersome graphical user interfaces.

Easy installation and management of packages is a Linux feature that becomes highly useful- master it to improve your experience. There is a third method of installing packages, and it involves downloading and launching .deb files from the Internet. Some software are bundled in that format, and they act similar to .exe files in that they just need to be double clicked to begin the installation process.

More Terminal Commands

Here are a few more basic terminal commands that you should internalize and put to use in your system. Fully understanding the basics will provide a decent foundation upon which to build on later.

- cp – "cp image1.jpg image2.jpg" – copies (and renames) the first parameter to the second supplied parameter. Copy directories with the –r switch.

- mv – "mv cat.jpg /home/Pictures" – Move the specified file to the given directory.

- shutdown – "shutdown –h now" – shuts down the computer. –h is a tag meaning "halt", but you can also use –r to restart. Now refers to the time until it executes.

- date – "date" – Displays the current date and time.

- free – "free –g" – Show the current RAM usage of programs.

- du – "du –h" – Give the HDD usage.

- ps – "ps" – Show the active processes using CPU time.

- touch – "touch memo.txt" – Used to create a new blank file in the current directory with the specified name.

- ifconfig – "ifconfig" – The Linux equivalent of ipconfig, it shows network information.

Some commands have "tags" or "switches" associated with them. These are the letters preceded by dashes. They all do different things, and learning which switches to use for what purpose is best found through that command's manual pages. See the advanced section for opening the manual.

One of the most useful programs from the command line, nano is a simple text editor that can be used to edit files and quickly make changes to settings or scripts. It is accessed by typing "nano" into a command line. You can type a file as needed and then press ctrl+x to save and quit. As you save, you will give it the name and file extension associated with it; notes.txt will create a text file with the name "notes". Alternatively, you can edit a file by typing "nano notes.txt". In that example, we open notes in the editor and display its contents in an editable state.

Nano may be very simple, but it is undoubtedly powerful and a time saver for quick changes and file creation.

Connecting to Windows / Mac Computers

Windows and OSX computers have built-in networking functions such as workgroups, domains, shares, and more. Integrating Linux computers into the network infrastructure that has been dominated by Windows server computers is fairly easy, though, and correct setup will allow you to see Windows shares as well as join corporate domains.

The first step to intercommunication is installing the "samba" package. Either find it through the software center, or type in "sudo apt-get install samba" to obtain and install the necessary software.

Sharing files from your Ubuntu machine to other computers involves creating a samba share. Samba runs off of the same protocols that other popular file sharing methods use, so files shared from the Ubuntu machine can easily be seen on Windows. After installing samba, use "sudo nano /etc/samba/smb.conf" to start editing the configuration file. At the very bottom of the file add these lines:

[share]

comment = File Share from Ubuntu

path = /srv/samba/share

browsable = yes

guest ok = yes

read only = no

create mask = 0755

Now, create the folder specified in "path" (sudo mkdir -p /srv/samba/share) and set permissions (sudo chown nobody:nogroup /srv/samba/share/) so that anybody can access its contents. Place any files you want to share within that directory, and then restart the service (sudo restart smbd, sudo restart nmbd) to make the share active. Lastly, log on to your other computer and navigate to the network shares. In Windows, they will appear in the left panel of file explorer. If the share does not appear automatically, type the IP into the file path box (find Ubuntu IP with ifconfig). You are now able to access Ubuntu's files from other operating systems.

You might also need to see files from other operating systems in the Ubuntu computer. Firstly, open the Ubuntu file explorer. From the menu bar, click "files", and then select "connect to server". In the resulting box, type the URL of the share you wish to access. It could be an ftp address (ftp://ftp.test.com), an http address (http://test.com), or a share address (smb://share/Folder). Without any additional hardware or setup, you can see the files this way.

Finally, joining a domain such as Active Directory allows your computer to interact with other operating systems on the network and achieve other business-oriented tasks. Whether you have a small home network, or whether you are adding Linux computers to a corporate domain, the process is the same. Install a few extra packages (realmd, sssd, sssd-tools, samba-common, samba-common-bin, samba-libs, krb5-user, adcli, packagekit). While installing them, it will ask for your domain name. Enter it in all caps. Enter "kinit -V adminname" replacing that with an actual admin account name in the domain. After entering the password you will have been authenticated to the domain. Now joining it is done with "realm --verbose join -U adminmame domainname.loc".

If it fails, it means the DNS is misconfigured on our device. Type "echo 'ad_hostname = nix01.domainname.loc' >> /etc/sssd/sssd.conf", then "echo 'dyndns_update = True' >> /etc/sssd/sssd.conf" and finally use "service sssd restart" to restart with those new settings. The first line sets the FQDN of our computer, so the line needs to be changed according to our domain settings. After a successful restart with correctly configured settings the terminal will claim it has joined the domain. Test this with "realm list". Now connected to AD you can administer the Linux device from your server!

For most users, however, creating shares and joining domains is far beyond the connectivity needs. Simple file sharing is much better done through USB drive transfers or a service such as Dropbox. Indeed Dropbox can be installed on the big three operating systems and files can be synced between them with no additional setup. On Ubuntu either download the .deb file directly from the website, install it from the software center, or use "sudo apt-get install nautilus-dropbox" to obtain the application. Within the Dropbox folder, place any files that you wish to transfer between computers and it will automatically be downloaded and updated on all other Dropbox computers you own.

Using other operating systems is not complicated when you connect them together. So long as the computers are on the same network you can create file shares, join them into a domain, or use a simple service such as Dropbox.

Useful Applications

Here is a list of the best Applications for your Ubuntu system that will help you get the most out of your computer.

- Office Productivity – Abiword, VI, Emacs, LibreOffice, nano

- Multimedia – VLC, DeaDBeef, Cmus, AquaLung, MPlayer, Miro

- Web Browsing – Firefox, Chromium, Midori, W3M

- Creativity – Aud

- acity, GIMP

- Other – Kupfer, Thunderbird, qBittorrent

And for programs that help with usability, there are so many varied choices that it depends on what you are trying to accomplish. The best way to discover a program is to search on the internet for a functionality you wish to add. For example, if you are searching for a quick way to open and close the terminal you might come across the program "Guake". Or if you are wanting audio within the terminal it might recommend "Cmus". Finding the perfect applications for you is part of the customization aspect of Linux, and it makes every install a little more personal for each user.

Administration

If you are looking for a "Control Panel" of sorts, you can find shortcuts to administrative tools such as network, printing, keyboard, appearance, and more from within the "System Settings" application. Some Ubuntu variants use "Settings Manager" or just "Settings" for the same purpose.

After launching it there will be links to other default configuration applications; just click on whichever you need to change to obtain a GUI for settings a few options. But not everything administrative is found through the GUI. Most low-level settings are only available through the command line, and as such you will need to know exactly what to type to edit them.

As an example, adding a new user to Ubuntu requires the "adduser" command. By following the command with a username, the terminal will prompt for basic information and a password. Setting that new user to be an administrator is done with "usermod -aG sudo nameofuser". Moreover a user can be deleted with "deluser". These options are difficult to find through GUI but can be done in seconds with a terminal.

"Task Manager", or the administration of running applications within Ubuntu is done through the terminal as well. The program "top" is standardly installed on all distributions (mostly), and starting it displays a list of all currently running processes as per task manager. By default though, the list of processes will be updated and moving around in such a way that it might be difficult to read the data we need. Press the "f" button to bring up a sorting list, navigate to "PID" with the arrow keys and press "s" to set over that option. Now use escape to return to top and we can now scroll through the list with page-up and page-down to view the tasks. Say, for instance, we want to close the program "Pidgin" because it is unresponsive. Find it in the list (or search for it with the above filtering commands) and take note of the PID (Process ID) number. Press "q" to quit top, then type "kill 4653" obviously replacing the number with the PID. At any time within top you can press "h" to see a list of keyboard shortcuts for various actions. If top is too difficult to use consider installing "htop", a "human readable" version of the program. It actually shows neat ASCII graphs detailing CPU, RAM, and other usage statistics. Search for a program with F3, then use F9 and Enter to kill it.

As for services, you might have noticed we use the "service" command to change their status. So starting a web server would be done with "service apache2 start", restarting it done by replacing start with restart, and stopping it by replacing start with stop. Finding a list of services is done with "service --status-all". Services are daemons, or background tasks that are continuously running. They can be gathering data, running a service such as Bluetooth and Wi-Fi, or waiting for user interaction.

Security Protocols

Linux has a focus on security in general, which contributes to its use in corporate and server settings. Taking advantage of the security protocols means that you are more secure than other operating systems and less likely to have your computer compromised. This requires good security principals, of course, and always being safe online. A computer without a password is hardly protected at all.

One feature brought over from UNIX is file permissions. Every file has a set of permission- the owner, group, and rights. The command "chown" changes the owner of a file, "chgrp" changes the group, and "chmod" changes the rights associated with the file. Discovering the permissions of a file or folder is done by typing "ls -l filename". It will return an initially confusing line such as "- rw- rw- r--". "R" means read, "W" stands for write, and the third option is "X" for execute. The three sets are respectively owner, group, and other. So our example file above has read and write permissions set for the owner and its group, but only read permissions for other users. This means that the owner and the group he belongs to (most likely sudo users) have permission to both access the file and change its contents, but other users on the network or PC can only view the contents and not edit it. Script files will need to have the X in order to be executed, and without it they cannot be run.

Most people will only need to use the "chmod" command to change the permissions of files they wish to use. We use the command and a set of numbers to set the permission of the file. "chmod 777 test.sh" makes the file readable, writable, and executable by all users anywhere because each specification (owner, group, other) has the number 7 attached to it. Numbers determine the permissions that entity has, and the number used is calculated like so:

- Start with the number 0.

- Add 4 for adding readability.

- Add 2 for write-ability.

- Add 1 for executable-ness.

- The number you have left determines the permissions.

6 would be read/write, but 1 would only be executable. 5 would be readable and executable, but not changeable. In our 777 example, we set owner, group, and others to all be 7. This is not particularly good security, because that means anybody anywhere can mess with that file. A more conservative permission set would be 775. Use security permissions advantageously for secure computing.

Security within Linux expands beyond just permissions. Ensure that you practice good security practices, and that you are following common sense in regards to security- install only needed programs, do not follow all internet advice, do not use sudo too often, use passwords, use encrypted networks, keep software up to date, encrypt important files, and make regular backups. As a final word of advice, look into using a distribution with SELinux, a module that supports AC and other security policies.

Scripting

Bash is the "programming language" or the terminal. When we type a command, we are doing so within bash. A script is a list of bash commands that execute in order, meaning we can create a script with a list of commands and run it to save time or automate terminal tasks that we normally have to type. As an intermediate and advanced Linux administrator, you can use scripts to greatly shorten the amount of work required for repetitive or constantly running tasks.

To start a script, create a new file "script.sh" within nano. The first line must always be "#!/bin/bash" to mark it as a bash script. Type the following lines for your first script.

echo "What is your name?"

read name

echo "Hey, $name. Here is your current directory, followed by the files."

Pwd

Ls

Save the script. Now we have to set the permissions to allow it to be run. Use "sudo chmod 777 script.sh", and then run the script with "./script.sh". So long as you copied the script exactly, it will ask for your name and then show you your directory and files. Take the concept and expand it further in your own scripts. You can run commands from installed programs as well, so you can write a script that automatically joins a domain, or one that connects to the network specified. Shutting down remote computers is a great automatic task as well.

Scripts can either be run manually or set to execute at certain times. To run a certain script every time the user logs in, open the "startup applications" program from dash and create a new app with the script as the source. Now every time that user logs in the script will run automatically. This is useful for setting up certain options or starting background services without requiring the user to do it themselves.

Scheduling tasks for a certain time can be done with the Cron system daemon. It is installed be default on some systems, but if not "sudo apt-get install cron" can be used. Start the service with "service cron start" and create a new crontab file with "crontab - e". Select nano as your text editor. At the bottom of the created file, add a new line with our scheduled task. The format goes as follows:

minute, hour, day, month, weekday, command

And we format it with these options to specify when to run the command. Time numbers start with 0, so the hours range from 0 to 23 and minutes are from 0 to 59. Replace any option with an asterick to specify that it will run on any value. Pay attention to these examples:

```
0 12 * * * ~/script.sh
```

This will run the script.sh found in the Home directory every day at noon.

```
30 18 25 12 * /usr/bin/scripts/test.sh
```

And this will run test.sh within the /usr/bin/scripts directory at 6:30 on Christmas day every year.

Conclusively, scripting and automating scripts are fantastic ways to take administrative control of regularly occurring tasks. Continue writing scripts, or look up examples online to see how your computing experience can be made easier with bash.

Advanced Terminal Concepts

Mastering Linux comes down to intimate comprehension of the tools available in the OS and how to utilize them. Many of the topics discussed in this chapter will focus on more tasks and how to accomplish them, or a few QOL improvements to the OS in general.

Compression and decompression of files often confuses Linux beginners. The tools are typically already installed, but the command line must be used. Furthermore, the strange .tar and .gz file-types are Linux-specific formats that you might often come across. All files can be unzipped or zipped with the gzip tool. Preinstalled on Ubuntu, we access it with the "tar" command. To compress a folder and the files contained within, navigate to it in terminal and type "tar – czvf name.tar.gz foldername". C stands for "create", z means "compress (gzip)", v is for "verbose", and f allows filename specification. If you want more compression (but at the cost of time), zip the folder with gzip2 by replacing the –z switch with the –j switch instead.

Now extracting that same archive can be done with "tar –xzvf name.tar.gz". You will notice that the –c was replaced with an –x, and this indicates extraction. Once again if you are dealing with bzip2 files use the –j switch instead.

Continuing with advanced terminal concepts, let us talk about a few quality tips and tricks that can save you time in the terminal. When typing a command or file name, press tab halfway through. This feature, tab completion, will guess what you are attempting to type and fill in the rest of the phrase. For files it will complete the name as shown in the directory, or complete a command by considering what you are trying to do. Linux experts and anyone that has to use the terminal regularly may seem as though they are typing exactly what they want with extreme accuracy and speed, but they are actually just using tab completion.

Users, especially administrators, will spend a decent amount of time with the sudo command because their instructions require elevated privileges to run. But when typing out a long command and forgetting to type sudo, you will be angered at having to type it again. Instead simply type "sudo !!", shorthand for "super user do again". It generously saves from typing an entire command again.

Another method of repeating commands is to use the up and down arrows. Pressing up continuously cycles through previously typed commands. You can also edit the commands with the left and right arrows to change the text contained within.

And the most requested terminal tip involves copy and pasting. Attempting to paste a line into the terminal results in the strange character ^v. The keyboard shortcut is not configured to work in the terminal, and that is why the strange combination is displayed. To actually paste, right click and select the option; or use the key combination shift+insert. Copy in the same way, but with ctrl+insert instead. While it might be okay to copy and paste terminal commands from the Internet (provided you understand the risk and know what they are doing in the command), do not try to paste from this publication. The formatting introduced through the medium in which you are reading it might have inserted special characters that are not recognized by the terminal, so it is best if you do not copy and paste, but rather you should type manually any commands presented.

Linux has a hidden feature that not many users know about. Files are displayed to the user when you visit that directory or type ls, but actually not all of the files are viewable this way. In Linux if you name a file with a period as the first character it will be marked as hidden. Hidden files are not normally visible by common users, and it acts as a way to protect configuration files from accidental editing/deleting/so forth. To see those files, we only need to add the − a tag to our ls search. In the GUI press ctrl+h in a directory to reveal the secret content. And as you create scripts and other configuration files consider hiding them with the period as a form of user protection.

Any command within terminal can be interrupted or quit with the ctrl+d key combination. Use it to stop a lengthy process or to exit out of a program/command that you do not understand.

Aliasing is a way to create your own personal shortcuts within the terminal. Instead of typing a long command or a bunch of smaller commands aliases can be used to combine them into a single user defined option. Just as the name implies, aliases are different names for anything you specify. Every alias is contained within a hidden config file- begin editing it with "nano ~/.bashrc". Because it exists within the user's home directory every alias will be pertinent only to that user. At the bottom of the file we can begin creating alias as per the following example:

```
alias gohome='cd ~ && ls'
```

This alias will change the directory to home and display the contents by typing "gohome". When creating aliases you must follow the formatting presented above exactly, meaning there is no space between the command and the equal sign. Multiple commands are strung together inside the single quotes separated by "&&". For more robust aliases, add a function instead. The following example combines cd and ls into a single command.

```
function cdls () {

    cd "$@" && ls
}
```

After writing your aliases, save the file and restart the computer. Your new commands are then available for use.

That file we edit, .bashrc, is the configuration file for the Ubuntu terminal. Besides making aliases we can also use it to customize our terminal settings, such as color, size, etc... A quick tip is to uncomment the "#force_color_prompt=yes" by removing the # and ensuring "yes" is after the equals. This adds color to the terminal, making certain words different colors. More options are available when you open a terminal, right click on it, and select profiles followed by profile preferences. Through the tabs here you can customize the font, size, colors, background colors, and much more. Customization of the terminal is recommended if you are going to be using it a lot, because it helps to be comfortable with the tools you will work with.

I/O Redirection

During normal terminal command execution, "normal input" (typed by the user, or read from a file/attribute/hardware) is entered and parsed by the command. Sometimes the command has "standard output" as well, which is the return text shown in the terminal. In "ls", the standard input is the current working directory, and the standard output is the contents of the folder.

Input and output are normally direct, but by using I/O redirection we can do more with the terminal. As an example, the "cat" command (concatenate) followed by a file will output that file to the screen. Running cat by itself opens a parser where any line that is input will be immediately output (use ctrl+d) to quit. But with I/O redirection hotkeys (<, >, <<, >>, |) we can redirect the output to another source, such as a file. And "cat > test.txt" will now put the standard output in that new file. Double signs signify appending, so "cat >> test.txt" will place the output at the end of the file rather than erasing the contents at the beginning.

The vertical line character, or the "pipe", uses another form of I/O redirection to take the output of one command and directly insert it into the input of another. "ls | sort –r" would take the output of ls and sort it into a backwards list. We redirected the output and gave it to another command to accomplish this.

And finally, the "grep" command is used very often within I/O redirection. Grep can search for a certain string within a specified file and return the results to standard output. Using redirection, this output can be put into other commands. An interesting feature of Linux to note is that object is a file, even hardware. So our CPU is actually a file that stores relevant data inside of it, and we can use grep and other tools to search within it. That example is fairly advanced, but here is a simpler instance:

"grep Conclusion report.txt"

And it will search within the file for that specific word. I/O redirection can become a complicated process with all of the new symbols and commands, but it is a feature that you can incorporate into your scripts and daily use that often allows for certain features and functions of Linux to be done in a single line.

Linux and the terminal are difficult concepts to fully master. But with practice and continuing dedication you will be able to perform masterful feats of computing and do helpful tasks that are not possible in Windows or OSX. Learning more about commands and how to use them certainly helps in this regard, so persist in your studies of new commands and their use. Positively the only command you actually need to memorize is "man", a command that will show the manual pages and documentation of any other command specified. The manual pages show switches, examples, and the intended use of every command on your system. Use the tool to your advantage and gain intimate knowledge of your system.

More Linux Information

To continue learning about Linux and the possibilities it can provide, consider the examples in this section. It will briefly discuss more uses for Linux, and a few other concepts that have yet to be talked about.

The "Linux file system" refers to the main layout of the files and folders on your computer. If you continue to "cd .." in the terminal, or if you click the back button on the GUI until it goes no further you will stumble upon the "root" directory. The folders here, bin, boot, etc, usr, and so on are how your hardware and settings are configured. Each folder has a specific purpose and use, and you can understand them by exploring the contents. As an example, user data is stored in home, but user programs are stored in usr. Because of how diverse and complicated the file system actually is it will not be discussed here, but if you wish to learn more do an Internet search or read the documentation associated with your operating system.

Linux systems are often used for purposes other than desktop use. Dedicated machines run variants of Linux because of the power and stability it provides. Even our cars have a Linux kernel running to keep track of error codes and help mechanics.

Servers often have Linux installed because of reliability and the functions the distributions have within them. For instance, Linux machines are used as firewalls because the "iptables" application provides excellent port blocking and intelligent filtering. You yourself can run a firewall on your system with the application as well, thus gaining business-level software for free. In this way, Linux is also great for networking. The machine can act as a switch, router, DNS server, DHCP server, and more just by installing the relevant applications.

And finally, Linux systems are not limited to the interfaces we have seen insofar. Every distro has its preferred desktop environment, but the interface can be extremely customized to the individual's preference. There are even file and web browsers for the terminal, which is greatly helpful for those using SSH or remote computing. All-in-all, you should try out different DE's by installing them and configuring them to your liking.

What Next and Conclusion

How you continue depends on what you want to do with your Linux distribution. For casual browsing and simple use, continue with Ubuntu and install the programs you need. For more adventurous people, consider installing a new distribution to see what each has to offer. Those wishing to learn even more deeply about Linux can install one such as Arch or DSL to build their own unique OS from scratch. Administrators and power users can install a server version of a distro to build their own Linux network, or they can consider changing over their environment from other operating systems to entirely free ones.

Conclusively, Linux is a powerful and relatively easy to use set of operating systems. But their real potential comes from the hard-to-master terminal and command line functions. Thank you for reading this publication, and I hope that it has shed some light on the mysterious subject of the defacto alternative operating system.

If Linux has confused you or did not live up to expectations, I implore you to take a second look at the features it can offer. While it may not have the same caliber of games or 3rd party proprietary software, the OS is simple and customizable enough to be used as a primary OS with maybe Windows or OSX as a secondary OS. Alternatives exist for just about every program, so if it is possible to get rid of Microsoft and Apple entirely, it is highly recommended you do so. Thank you again, and make good use of your new Linux knowledge.

Related Titles

Hacking University: Freshman Edition Essential Beginner's Guide on How to Become an Amateur Hacker

Hacking University: Sophomore
Edition. Essential Guide to Take
Your Hacking Skills to the Next
Level. Hacking Mobile Devices,
Tablets, Game Consoles, and Apps

Hacking University: Junior Edition.
Learn Python Computer Programming
From Scratch. Become a Python Zero to
Hero. The Ultimate Beginners Guide in
Mastering the Python Language

Hacking University: Senior Edition Linux. Optimal Beginner's Guide To Precisely Learn And Conquer The Linux Operating System. A Complete Step By Step Guide In How Linux Command Line Works

Hacking University: Graduation Edition.
4 Manuscripts (Computer, Mobile,
Python, & Linux). Hacking Computers,
Mobile Devices, Apps, Game Consoles
and Learn Python & Linux

Data Analytics: Practical Data Analysis and Statistical Guide to Transform and Evolve Any Business, Leveraging the power of Data Analytics, Data Science, and Predictive Analytics for Beginners

C++: Learn C++ Like a Boss. A Beginners Guide in Coding Programming And Dominating C++. Novice to Expert Guide To Learn and Master C++ Fast

About the Author

Isaac D. Cody is a proud, savvy, and ethical hacker from New York City. Currently, Isaac now works for a mid-size Informational Technology Firm in the heart of NYC. He aspires to work for the United States government as a security hacker, but also loves teaching others about the future of technology. Isaac firmly believes that the future will heavily rely computer "geeks" for both security and the successes of companies and future jobs alike. In his spare time, he loves to analyze and scrutinize everything about the game of basketball.

www.ingramcontent.com/pod-product-compliance
Lightning Source LLC
Chambersburg PA
CBHW071149050326
40689CB00011B/2043